Isabel McNeill Carley Orff Essentials Collection

Recorder Improvisation and Technique

BOOK THREE

Advanced - Composing, Arranging, Analysis

Classroom or Lesson Setting

Isabel McNeill Carley

Second Edition
Teacher and Student

B P
Brasstown Press
Charlottesville, VA
brasstownpress.com

Printed in USA
ISBN 978-0-9836545-2-0

Acknowledgments

Edited and produced by Brasstown Press with production assistance from Ayla Palermo.

Redesign of cover and symbols by Browning Porter Design.

Note on the second edition

This newly designed and reset edition of **Recorder Improvisation and Technique Book Three** (**RIT Three**) retains the contents of the first edition, with the addition of expanded reference and resource materials.

Reviews of this Edition

In 12 lessons, Carley deftly guides the player through scales, melodic ornamentation, decoration of the third, canons, chord changes, descant creation and free improvisation. She includes many fine musical examples, but the focus is the emphasis on improvisation leading to composition in the forms that parallel the history of Western music. [The three RIT books]contain a wealth of practical pedagogy for learning and teaching recorder—a reflection of Carley's incomparable musicianship and extensive work with children and adults in ensemble settings. These new editions enable access to this unique approach to developing recorder technique through improvisation.

~ **Leslie Timmons** in *American Recorder*

Book Three would be an excellent resource for Grades 7 and 8, and even secondary school programmes, and will be very inspiring for knowledgeable and experienced Schulwerk teachers. The modes, introduced in Book Two, are further explored. Functional harmony is introduced, as are the natural, melodic and harmonic scales. Lesson 3 includes a discussion about musical style in the Renaissance and Baroque periods, with opportunities for students to experiment with ornamentation and variation. Lesson 11 is about making descants, and Lesson 12 features "improvisation for Movement," and "accompanying movement."

All three [RIT] books have some of the most concise, well-organised and helpful indexes I have ever seen. The lessons referenced include the focus of the lesson, what is introduced, which recorder voices are used and the titles of the music. All three books include language directed at both the Teacher and the Student(s). Each of the new edition books has an expanded reference and resource section at the back.

~ **Kim Kendrick** in *Ostinato*

Comments on previous editions of Recorder Improvisation and Technique

Your recorder books are excellent ... completely in the spirit of the Schulwerk.

~ **Gunild Keetman**, co-creator, with Carl Orff, of the Orff Schulwerk

The tunes are lovely, and even the patterns are satisfying.

~ **Miriam Samuelson**, founding member of the American Orff-Schulwerk Association

Isabel Carley has given us a guide to musicianship. The recorder is only the means.

~ **Elizabeth Nichols**, founding member of the American Orff-Schulwerk Association

CONTENTS

Major Scales & their Related Modes

	Major • *Do*	Aeolian • *La*	Dorian • *Re*	Phrygian • *Mi*	Mixolydian • *So*
C	CDEFGABC	ABCDEFGA	DEFGABCD	EFGABCDE	GABCDEFG
G	GABCDEF♯G	EF♯GABCDE	ABCDEF♯GA	BCDEF♯GAB	DEF♯GABCD
F	FGAB♭CDEF	DEFGAB♭CD	GAB♭CDEFG	AB♭CDEFGA	CDEFGAB♭C
D	DEF♯GABC♯D	BC♯DEF♯GAB	EF♯GABC♯DE	F♯GABC♯DEF♯	ABC♯DEF♯GA
B♭	B♭CDEFGAB♭	GAB♭CDE♭FG	CDE♭FGAB♭C	DE♭FGAB♭CD	FGAB♭CDE♭F

Hand Signs

Do' = 

[eye level]

Ti =

La =

So =

Fa =

Mi =

Re =

Do =

[waist height]

Instruments & Abbreviations

Recorders

Nino	Sopranino Recorder
SR	Soprano Recorder
AR	Alto Recorder
TR	Tenor Recorder
BR	Bass Recorder

Percussion

HD	Hand Drum
FC	Finger Cymbals
Ti	Timpani
Tr	Triangle
Tam	Tambourine

Pitched Percussion (Orff Instruments)

SG	Soprano Glockenspiel
AG	Alto Glockenspiel
SX	Soprano Xylophone
AX	Alto Xylophone
BX	Bass Xylophone
SM	Soprano Metallophone
AM	Alto Metallophone
BM	Bass Metallophone

Stringed Instruments

Gtr	Guitar
Bs	Bass
Vc	Violoncello (or bass krummhorn or organ)
Bor	Bordun (or Cello)

Introduction

Recorder Improvisation and Technique Book Three (**RIT Three**) is packed with discovery. First, though, it does assume proficiency in playing both alto and soprano recorders. Prior mastery of **RIT One** and **RIT Two** is recommended, though competent players will find these lessons directly accessible, if challenging, as the book stands on its own. By the end, this short book also belies its title. It is not so much about the recorder, per se. Improvisation has led to musical composition, and technique can be taken for granted. It is a thrilling ride.

Many enthusiastic teachers and recorder players are comfortable with improvising, but may be intimidated by the thought of writing music. Here is an approach that bridges that gap. Not to transform everyone into a composer, mind you, but to embrace the joy of music-making with the confidence and freedom that spring from deep understanding.

As early as the 1970s, at Barbara Grenoble's Orff Certification courses at the University of Denver, Isabel Carley taught composition in the Orff style, along with recorder and improvisation. This book is the closest approximation in print to those classes. Already a published composer when she studied composition with Carl Orff in Austria in 1963, she knew what she was doing. She wanted to share it.

Now, thirty-four years since it was originally published, the capstone of her legacy, **RIT Three**, is back in print. Built from a synthesis of Orff and Keetman's creative genius, the materials of Medieval, traditional and improvised music, and Carley's own integrative insights, the result is genuine and inspiring. That hallmark Orff-Schulwerk sound - an amalgam of Indonesian, African, and pre-Classical European sources - here mixes with North American traditions, Carley's original pieces, and each student's creativity, to form wholly original music.

Along the way, the book covers the diatonic modes, the minor scales, conventional I - IV - V harmony, organum, faux bourdon, descants, shifting chords, the Chaconne variation form, improvisation for the dance, and more. Throughout, students encounter songs to sing and play on recorders and Orff instruments, always refreshed by that infinitely renewable resource, improvisation.

Anne M Carley
Charlottesville, VA

Original Introduction to the First Edition

Recorder Improvisation and Technique Book Three, like its predecessors, is designed to parallel and to supplement the basic material in the Orff Schulwerk publications, and to spell out in detail how the sequence can be applied to recorder playing and teaching. The improvisational techniques that are developed here for recorders can, of course, be readily transferred to other instruments and to the voice.

Book Three expands the resources to include functional harmonic relationships in major, modal, and minor scales. The dominant is first introduced in major scales. Basses are matched to melodies, and melodies are improvised to match given basses or chord patterns. Subdominants are similarly introduced.

Historical techniques of melodic ornamentation and of paraphony are introduced and developed, including the use of organum, faux bourdon, heterophony, the decoration of the third, making decants, and improvising or composing chaconnes and other variation forms. A final chapter develops improvisation for movement, free solo improvisation, and various kinds of group improvisation. Many examples of early music and folk songs are included.

It is assumed that students already play both C and F recorders, and can switch from one fingering to the other as required. It is also assumed that students at this level will have completed a second standard instruction book for adults. Hence there are relatively few exercises for simply technical aims. The emphasis is always on improvisation, since it is the key to both musicianship and technical mastery.

Isabel Carley
Brasstown, NC
October 1977

Lesson 1

Review D Major
A Major
Finding basses for tunes
Improvising tunes for given basses
Chord patterns on recorders
Improvising over I - V chord patterns

This three-book **Recorder Improvisation and Technique** sequence follows the path of the Orff-Schulwerk Volumes. The materials of music are gradually and logically introduced. Parallelling Volume I, first comes the pentatonic in **RIT One**. Next major (Volumes II and III) and minor (Volumes IV and V) modes are presented in **RIT Two**, with bordun or drone accompaniments, then with moving borduns and ostinati, and finally with shifting chords. Cadential harmony comes only after a long development in the Orff-Schulwerk Volumes, as it did in the recent history of Western music. Similarly, **RIT Two** did not introduce cadential harmony until Lessons 12 and 13. Here, throughout this concluding book, we explore it more fully.

1. Play what you hear in the key of **D** Major: **D E F♯ D E F♯ • A B C♯ D** *etc.*

   Take turns with your practice partner as Teacher.

2. Practice ⓐ through ⓕ silently, paying particular attention to which fingers must be lifted in each combination.

   Then play, at various tempi, and with as much variety of tonguing as you can invent:

3. Improvise scale patterns in **D** Major for your partner or the class to echo, in the following meters, with at least two kinds of tonguing in each tune

   2/4

   3/4

   4/4

   6/8.

4. Practice the following arpeggio pattern as needed, gradually increasing your tempo.

5. On your Alto recorder, transpose the previous pattern to **G** Major by ear.

6. Transpose the previous arpeggios to **A** Major by ear, and write them below.

   Play them on your Alto, repeating as needed.

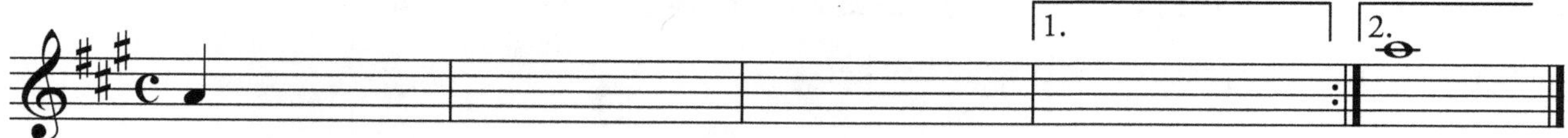

7. Play the following folk songs.

   - Then add the bass line for Tenor or Bass recorder on the second staff. Keep it as simple as possible, simply outlining the chord changes from **I** to **V** and back again.

   - Add a rhythm pattern on hand drum or tambourine if you wish.

Go Tell Aunt Nancy

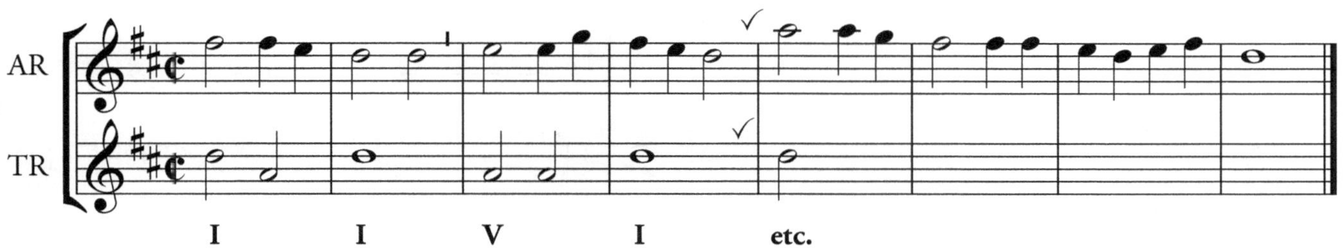

Did You Ever See A Lassie

8. Improvise melodies on your recorder over the following basses:

9. Write in the **I - V** chord shifts under the following tune:

10. Practice the following chord sequences

- As written
- In **G** Major
- In **F** Major.

Optionally, use a second Tenor recorder to substitute for a Bass recorder.

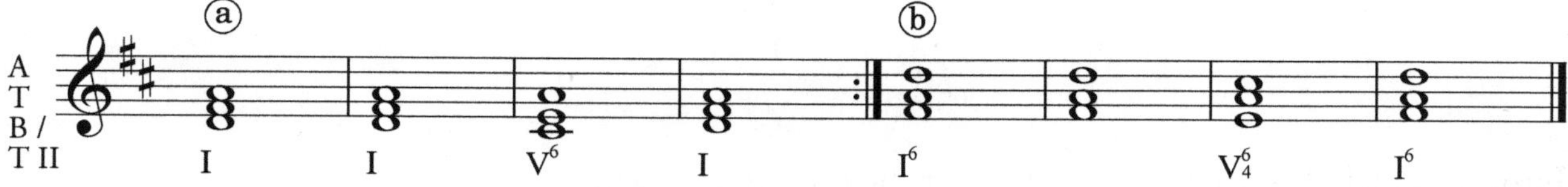

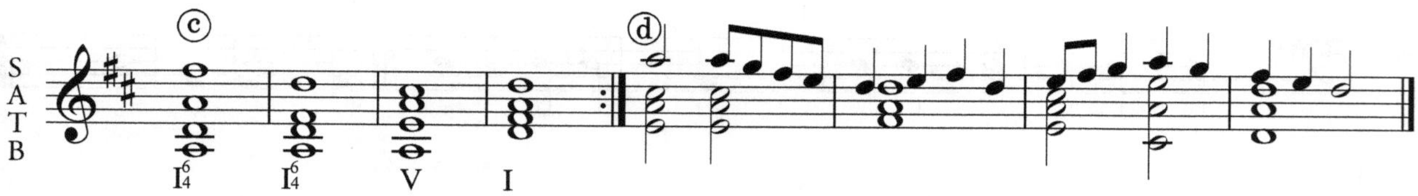

11. Over the following chord sequence

- Improvise a melody Q+A around the class
- Improvise a melody Q+A with your partner
- Improvise a melody by yourself
- Improvise a melody Q+A, Q+A with your partner
- Add a part for timpani or string bass *pizzicato.*

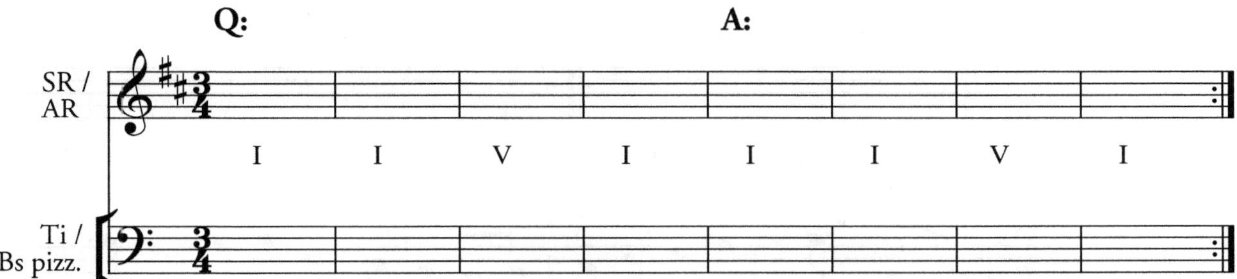

12. Take turns with your partner improvising tunes over AX or BX accompaniment patterns in various **I - V** chord sequences, such as

- **I - V - V - I**
- **V - I - V - I**
- **I - I - V - I.**

13. Work out a bass part to fit the following tune, using only **G** and **D**.

14. Into how many keys can you transpose **Nancy's Fancy**?
Try:

- **A** Major
- **B♭** Major
- **D** major (on an Alto recorder) and
- **C** Major.

Lesson 2

Transposition

Variation

Doubling in thirds and sixths

1. Echo play in the key of **A** Major in class, with your partner, and by yourself.

2. Improvise scale tunes in various meters for your partner or the class to echo. Notes may be repeated as needed to come out even, rhythmically.

3. Improvise Q+A phrases with your partner over these basses:

4. Play what you see, practicing as needed, at various tempi, and with different tonguings:

5. Practice the following familiar tune as needed.

   Then work out a bass for timpani, BX, or cello *pizzicato.*

   Add parts for unpitched percussion if you wish.

6. Transpose it to **B♭** and play as a three-part round, combining instruments in different octaves if you wish.

7. Work out a dance for Alto recorder and timpani in the key of **A.**

   Can you limit the range so that a Soprano recorder or a Tenor could also play the tune?

   Which notes will you use? _______

Dance for Alto Recorder and Timpani

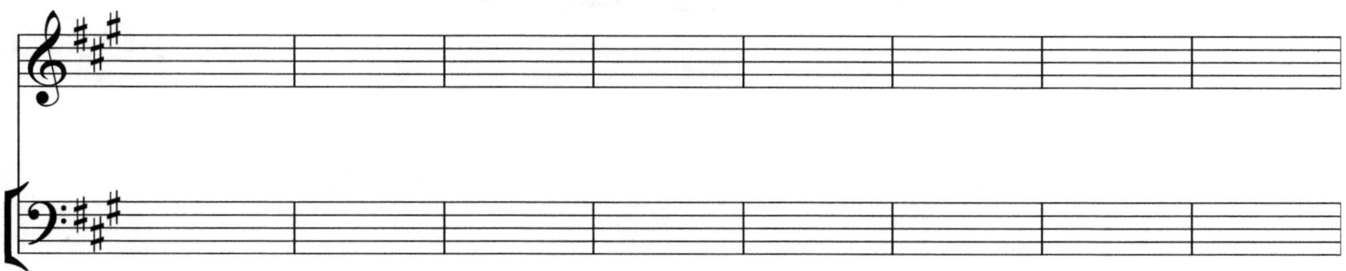

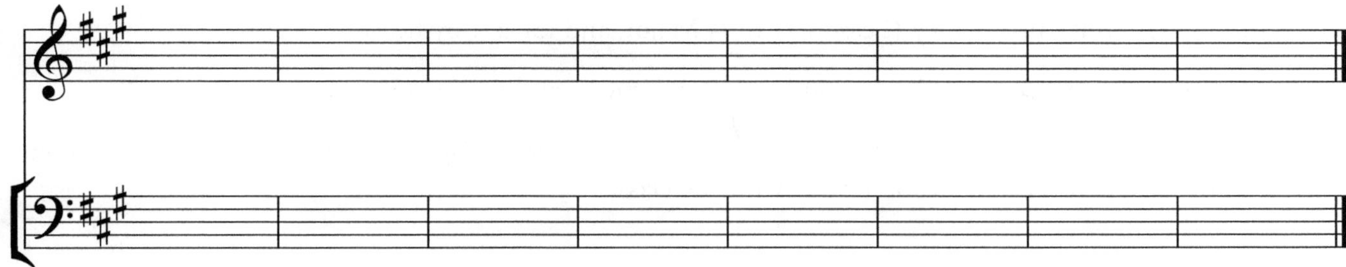

8. Write the appropriate chord numbers under the tune you just wrote, and take turns with your partner improvising a rhythmically interesting timpani part to match the chords. Limit yourself to I and V.

French Canadian Tune

French Canada

9. In how many keys can you play this tune?_________

   Which are easier on the Alto?_________

   Which on the Soprano?_________

10. Transpose **Go Tell Aunt Nancy (Lesson 1)** to **A** Major, and learn it by heart.
    - Then work out a set of variations on it, changing meter and mode as you see fit.
    - Work with your partner, one improvising variations, the other adjusting the bass part to fit, until you find two or three that you want to play for the class.

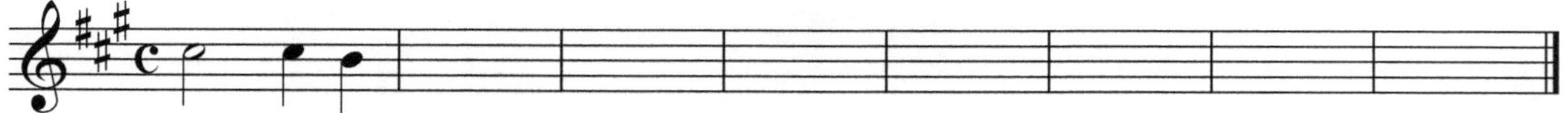

11. Practice the following chord patterns, paying close attention to your intonation.

- ***The third of the chord must always be high, the fifth slightly low.***
- ***<u>Think</u> each chord tone before you play it.***
- ***<u>Sing</u> with syllables as well, to be sure which scale tone you will be playing.***
- ***Practice all parts, on whichever recorders you have.***

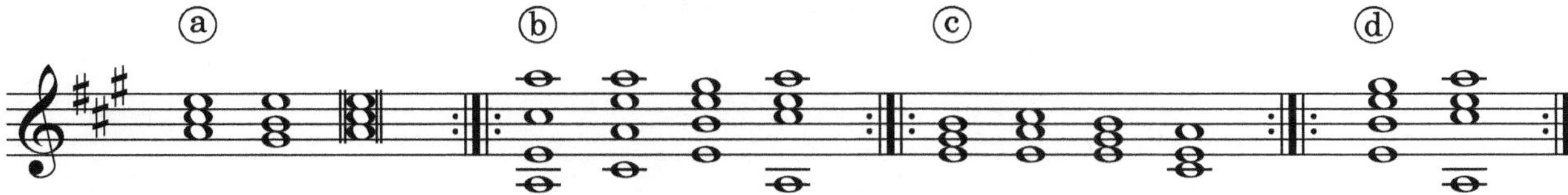

12. Practice the following scale exercises, again being particularly aware of your intonation. Add timpani parts to make them more interesting, and write the timpani parts in under the music.

Ti: ____

Ti: ____

13. Once the major scale is complete, many tunes lend themselves to doubling at the third or sixth.
    - Add a second part to the tune below (choose above or below the melody).
    - Indicate which recorders should play.
    - Notate the chord shifts.

French Lullaby

Lesson 3

Melodic ornamentation in historic styles
Melodic variations on a familiar folk tune

Melodic Ornamentation & Variation

Throughout the Renaissance and Baroque periods, musicians were expected to be able to decorate the bare bones of a tune spontaneously.

The melody might be played straight on the first statement, but each repetition was a challenge to the player's ingenuity and invention.

Ornamentation might be much or little, according to the style of the original tune and the competence of the player.

Primarily, it meant filling in the skips in the tune and inventing what the English composers of the time called "Divisions," stepwise elaborations of the tunes using smaller note values, such as in the following example, **Moriske**, where the composer Arbeau ornaments the [A] melody in the [B] section:

Moriske

Arbeau, 1589

1. Practice **Moriske** as needed. Then try making your own similar ornamented versions of the A section, being careful to maintain a steady beat so that the ornaments sound casual and easy.

2. Here is the first strain of another old French dance, **Branle de Champaigne,** with two possible ornamented versions, ⓐ and ⓑ, one quite simple, the other more elaborate.

   Practice as needed, until you get the feel of the style, and then improvise a couple more of your own.

   Note: Your own version will be most effective if you use only one or two characteristic figures in each version.

Branle de Champaigne

France

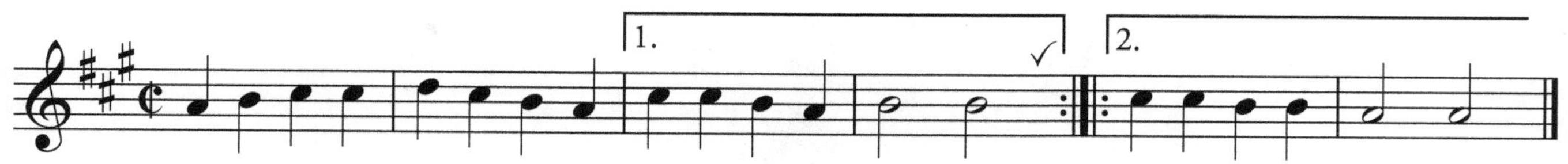

3. Decorate the following two dances, **Königstanz** and **Mohrentanz**, in the same way, playing them over and over till you find your own version.

Königstanz

Susato, 1551

Mohrentanz

Susato, 1551

4. After you are satisfied with your melodic variations on these two written dances, improvise a set of variations on a familiar folk song using the same type of ornamentation. Change the mode, too, if you wish.

Lesson 4

Natural, Melodic, Harmonic Minors
Minor scales of E, A, B, F♯
Combining short dances into longer forms

1. Once functional harmony with its **V - I** cadences became established in Western music, the minor modes were altered to allow for the raised seventh degree in the **V** chord. During the transition from modal music to a harmonic style, melodies were often ambiguous as far as the scale itself was concerned, and different composers would set the same tune with different harmonies and alter different notes of the tune accordingly.

   The Natural Minor scale matches exactly the key signature, and is the familiar Aeolian mode by another name. It is a *La* scale.

   With the key signature of **C** Major, what would be the natural minor scale? ________

   With key signature of **G** Major, what would its relative minor be? ________

   What notes would you find in the scale? ______________________________

   Write the Natural Minor scales below to match the key signatures in ⓐ and ⓑ:

ⓐ

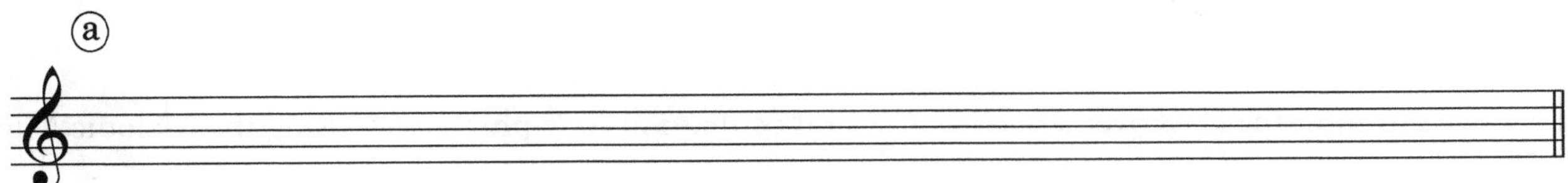

ⓑ

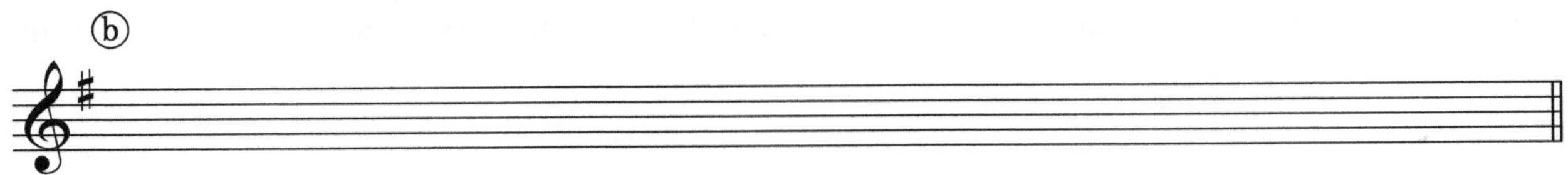

2. The Melodic Minor scale uses the raised fifth (*Fi*) and seventh (*Si*) degrees on a rising melodic line, and uses the lowered sixth and seventh on a descending tune, like the following scale.
   - Sing the syllables.
   - Then play, an octave higher.

Write the Melodic Minor scales below to match the key signatures:

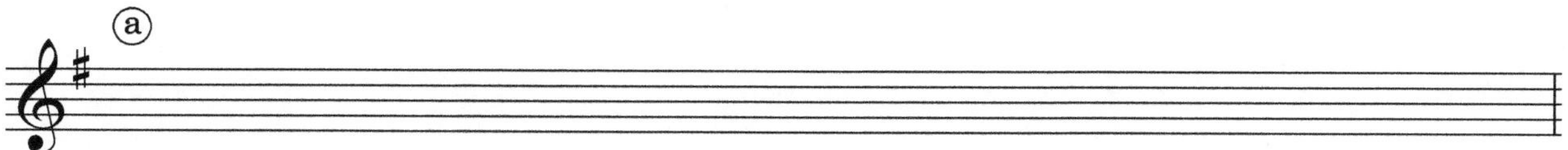

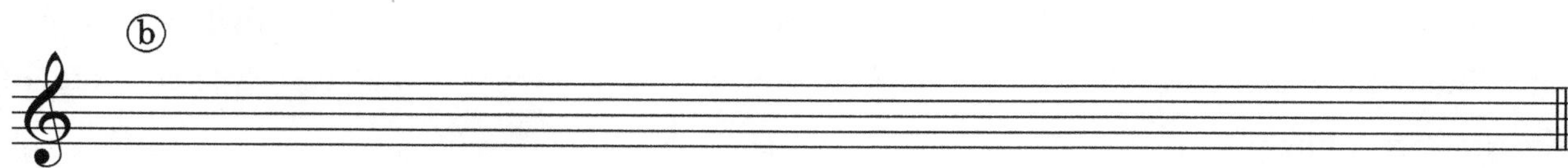

3. Echo what you hear in **B** Minor, using the Melodic Minor
   - With your partner
   - In class.

   Take turns being Teacher.

4. Improvise a slow, legato piece which you might use to accompany mirror movement, using whichever recorder you choose, in **B** minor.

5. Play Q+A around the class over a body-percussion ostinato in four-phrase sets, using the Melodic Minor in **B**.

   Again, repeating the question, with three people for each four-phrase set.

   Again, with only two people, each doing both Q and A, but number two repeating the first question.

6. The following two dances afford good examples of the use of the Melodic Minor scale. Memorize your favorite, and work out a drum part to fit:

Round Dance (Warum)

Susato, 1551

The Siege of Limerick

Playford, 17th c.

7. The Harmonic Minor scale simply borrows the raised seventh from the major scale to permit the usual **V - I** cadence.

   This leaves an awkward interval from the low sixth to the high seventh in the scale. Very often this interval is simply omitted in the melody itself.

   Practice the Harmonic Minor scales below, at different speeds and with a variety of tonguing.

   Then take turns improvising scale tunes for your partner or the class to echo.

8. Play Q+A with your partner or around the class using the Harmonic Minor scale on

   - **E** or
   - **B** or
   - **F♯**

   over a **I - I - V - V • I - I - V - I** accompaniment on BX, timpani, or recorders.

9. Work out a simple bass part for the following **Time-Change Dance**, using only the roots of the tonic and dominant chords.

   Add a part for hand drum, tambourine, or triangle.

   Try to make the bass part rhythmically interesting.

Time-Change Dance

Isabel Carley

B Minor Dance

10. Improvise a similar dance in **B** Minor over the following chord pattern for the bass
    - Solo
    - With a partner
    - With three recorders in different ranges
    - With a small group.

    At first, use mostly the chord tones themselves, and then gradually introduce more and more passing and neighboring tones in characteristic rhythm patterns to make the individual parts interesting.

11. Use one or another version of your **B Minor Dance** from Step 10 as the [B] section of a longer dance, using **Time-Change Dance** in Step 9 above as the [A] section.

    In the final statement of [A] you could add improvised parts under the tune and new unpitched percussion parts as well, if you wish.

    How many different forms can you work out using these two sections?

Lesson 5

Scale canons
Improvising a second part
Chords on recorder for improvisation
Improvised accompaniment

1. Play what you hear in **B♭** Major: **B♭ C D • F G A B♭ • B♭ C D E♭ • F G A B♭ C D** *etc.*
2. Echo scale patterns around the class in **B♭** Major, from **F** to **F'** and from **B♭** to **B♭'**, on both Soprano and Alto recorders.
3. Review the following combinations, and practice as needed:

4. Practice these scale canons at various tempi and with various tonguings:

5. Improvise a BX part to fit **The Paw-Paw Patch**. Then use the same bass part as the accompaniment for an improvised tune with the same essentially chordal melody. Write the chord names under the tune.

The Paw-Paw Patch

Chords:

6. Over a BX pattern similar to that above, improvise Q+A phrases around the class in the key of **B**♭. Add other ostinati if you wish, on either recorders or other barred instruments.

7. Play the following chord sequences, paying particular attention to your intonation.
   - Then take turns improvising a tune over the pattern of your choice, on the Soprano or Sopranino recorder.
   - Transfer the patterns to bar instrument(s) if there are not enough players to use recorders.
   - Name the chords.

8. Practice the following Fifteenth-Century carol tune until you know it by heart. Then take turns with your partner improvising a second part, doubling the tune in thirds and/or sixths. Write in your second part, either above or below the tune, in the space provided.

Unto Us A Child Is Born

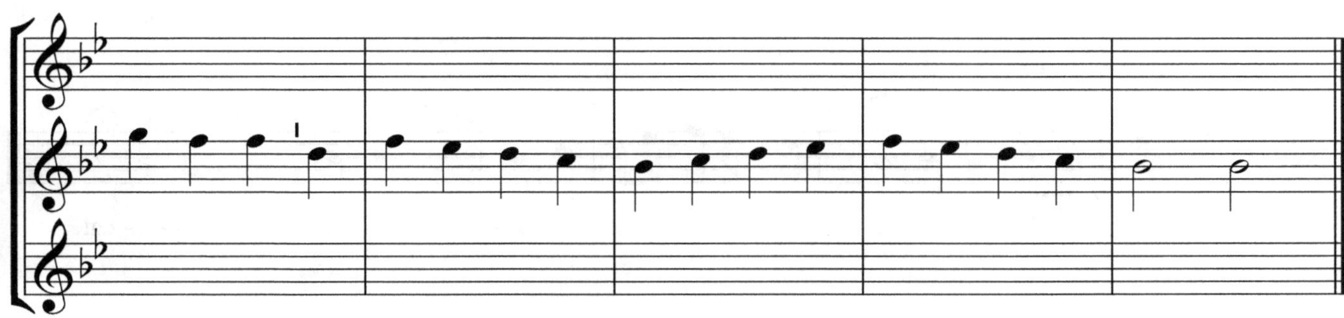

9. Practice **La Guignolée** on both **C** and **F** instruments until you can play it up to tempo. Work out a **I - V** part for BX or timpani, and write it below. If you wish, add a second part for another recorder. Specify which one.

La Guignolée

French Canadian

10. Practice the following three-part canon with both **C** and **F** recorders.

- Then work out the chord pattern on BX, timpani, or cello *pizzicato.*
- Add two or three complementary ostinati for barred instruments.
- Assign recorder parts and put it together.

Viva La Musica

Praetorius c. 1600

11. Play "Pass-it-on," one phrase each, over the following BX/AX ostinato patterns, in class and with your partner.

12. Again, in sets of four phrases, Q+A, Same Question + Different Answer

- In class, or
- With a partner, or
- By yourself.
- Make up your own **I - V** patterns if you prefer.

13. Practice the **Spring Canon**

- On your Alto by yourself
- In two-part canon with your partner, and
- In three-part canon in class.
- Write the chord symbols under the tune, and take turns improvising an appropriate accompaniment on BX or timpani.
- Add another melodic ostinato on the instrument of your choice, if you wish.

Spring Canon

German

Now ev - ery - one's sing - ing, and spring - time is spring - ing, And

14. You may recall the English dance tune, **Dick's Maggot,** from **RIT Two** Lesson 7, when you were learning **B♭**.

- Now analyze its harmonic structure.
- Play it on Alto recorder, adding BX accompaniment.

Dick's Maggot

Playford, 1703

Lesson 6

G Minor

Harmonic Minor scale patterns

Melodic improvisation over I - V chord patterns

The relative minor of B♭ Major is a *La* scale built on G.
When it corresponds exactly to the key signature, it is the Natural Minor scale, also called the Aeolian mode.

1. Sing the syllables in the scale below.
   Echo play with hand signs.
   Then play.

2. Echo play around the class, or with your partner.
   - Each person in turn improvises a short phrase in a given rhythm for the entire class to echo.
   - If the echo's not perfect, the leader must be prepared to repeat the phrase.
   - If the echo's correct, the next person improvises a new phrase in the same meter for the class to echo, without interruption.

3. In the Melodic Minor scale, both the sixth and seventh degrees are raised as the melody goes up, and lowered coming down. Notice the appropriate accidentals below.

   Practice the ascending scale in canon, and then the descending scale in canon, listening very critically that the resultant chords are in tune.

4. Take turns improvising scale tunes for the class to echo, going either up or down the scale, repeating single notes as needed to make a good tune.

   Again, using only the upper tetrachord (the diatonic notes comprising the perfect fourth down from high **G**), and remembering to use **E**♮ and **F**♯ going up and **F**♮ and **E**♭ coming down.

5. Here is the tune of one of Pierre Attaignant's pavanes. What is the scale? ________

   Practice as it stands.

   Then try decorating the melody with passing tones and neighboring tones, making "Divisions" as in Lesson 3.

Pavane

Attaignant, 16th c.

Try this Hand Drum part with it: HD

6. Here is a Seventeenth-Century version of **Greensleeves**.

   What is the scale? ________

Greensleeves and Yellow Lace

England, 17th c.

7. Here are two three-part canons by Antonio Caldara to play on Alto recorder.
   Practice your entrances and phrasing until they are smooth.
   What is the significance of the raised **F**'s?

Canon 1

Antonio Caldara

Canon 2

Antonio Caldara

8. Improvise with your partner in the Natural Minor and Melodic Minor over the following bass lines:

9. Improvise in the Melodic Minor on **G** over the following chord progressions played on the bar instruments of your choice.

   Use a variety of meters and tempi.

   Take turns with your partner in adapting the chords to different bar instruments and in inventing melodies.

   - **I - I - V - I**
   - **V - I - V- I**
   - **I - I - V - V | I - I - V - I**

10. Practice the following patterns in the Harmonic Minor, at various speeds, and with as much variety of tonguing as you can muster.

11. Practice the next two songs until they flow gracefully. The first, **Joy in the Gates**, can be sung and played as a six-part round. Listen to your intonation. The second, **Raisins and Almonds**, is a lullaby from the late Nineteenth Century.

Joy in the Gates

from Thomas Ravenscroft's Pamelia, England, 1609

Six-part round

Raisins and Almonds

Abraham Goldfaden (1840-1908)

12. Improvise answers to the following melodic questions, being careful to use the appropriate minor scale suggested by the question.

Lesson 7

Minors and Modes
Modal variations on a familiar tune
Variations on Q+A improvised tune
Parallel modes

Of the modes we have already learned, three are minor: the Aeolian, Dorian, and Phrygian scales.

The Aeolian is identical with the Natural Minor.

With the Melodic Minor and the Harmonic Minor, we now have five Minor scales.

Now we can use minor as well as major modes, and the minor scales, to work out sets of variations.

1. Practice the following minor tunes, **Portabella** and **The Beaux Stratagem**, as needed, and identify the scale in each example.

Portabella

English Country Dance Tune, c. 1715

What is the scale? ________

The Beaux Stratagem

English Country Dance Tune, c. 1707

What is the scale? ________

2. Echo play with your partner in each of the minor scales in turn: Aeolian, Dorian, Phrygian, Melodic Minor, and Harmonic Minor, with **E** as the tonal center.

   Spell each minor scale:

   - Aeolian **E F♯ G A B C D E**
   - Dorian **E F♯ G A B C♯ D E**
   - Phrygian **E** ____________________
   - Melodic Minor **E** ____________________
   - Harmonic Minor **E** ____________________

3. Choose a favorite simple folk song and play it in each of the five modes in a given major scale.

   For example, using the scale of **A** Major (Ionian, on *Do*):

   - Dorian would begin on **B** since it is a scale on *Re*
   - Phrygian would begin on **C♯** since it is a scale on *Mi*
   - Mixolydian would begin on **E** since it is a scale on *So*
   - Aeolian would begin on **F♯** since it is a scale on *La.*

4. With **E** as the tonal center, play Pass-it-on around the class using the minor scale of your choice.

5. Again, using a different minor scale.

6. Using the Harmonic Minor on **D** (**D E F G A B♭ C♯ D**), play Q+A around the class in four-phrase sets.

   Make your answers <u>longer</u> than the questions.

7. Again, Q+A, Same Q + Different A.

   Use **I - V - V - I** chord pattern played by xylophones.

   Write out your chordal patterns below:

8. Using a four-phrase Q+A tune from the class, or your own, work out three or four variations.

   For each variation

   - Change the mode, and
   - Retain the same tonal center.

9. Choose a mode and a tonal center.

   - Improvise scale melodies for the class or your partner to echo.
   - Use a variety of tonguing.

10. Using the same tune you chose for Step 3, work out a set of variations in Parallel Modes, *i.e.*, all starting on the same pitch.

    If **C** is the tonal center, what notes will you play in each of the following scales?

    - Major **C D E F G A B C**
    - Aeolian ______________________
    - Phrygian ______________________
    - Dorian ______________________
    - Melodic Minor ______________________
    - Harmonic Minor ______________________
    - Mixolydian ______________________

11. Pay attention to the harmonic possibilities as you learn the melody for **Garry Owen**.

Garry Owen

Irish-American Fiddle Tune

What is the scale in **Garry Owen**? _______

Can you find a shifting chord pattern to fit the tune?

Write in the appropriate chord numbers and take turns improvising an accompaniment on AX or BX, using three mallets.

12. Here are two scale canons
    - Sing them on solfège syllables
    - Play them.

    Take turns on each part, and listen very critically to the resultant chords.

    Play **Scale Canon 1** on Alto recorders.

Scale Canon 1

Three-part canon

Scale Canon 2

What is the scale in **Scale Canon 1**? _______

What is the scale in **Scale Canon 2**? _______

Can you change **Scale Canon 2** to the Melodic Minor? Which notes must be altered?

Lesson 8

Hand sign improvisation in parallel thirds
Adding improvised second parts to tunes
Organum
Faux Bourdon
Heterophony
Parallel thirds and sixths over a bass line
Shifting chords

1. Echo Teacher's phrases in **E** Dorian; in **B** Dorian.
   Take turns being the leader, four phrases each, without interruption.
   Be prepared to repeat any phrase if the class was unable to repeat it accurately.

2. Q+A around the class in **E** Aeolian; then **B** Aeolian over these accompanying patterns:

3. Follow Teacher's hand signs in **A** Aeolian.
   Again, in two parts, the lower part following the hand signs, the upper part following the stepwise motion of the lower part a third higher.
   Reverse parts.
   Practice with a few friends using both hands to indicate the pitches for each part.

4. Again, but the second part starts a sixth below the tune Teacher is leading with hand signs.
   Reverse parts.
   Try again using another tonal center.

5. The Europeans discovered centuries ago the pleasure of singing in parallel thirds and sixths. Here are two simple folk songs for you to add second parts to, using either thirds or sixths. The first one you may remember from **RIT One** Lesson 10:

A La Claire Fontaine

French Canadian

Yankee Doodle

United States

6. Write the appropriate chord numbers under the two tunes, and work out a simple chordal accompaniment on the instrument(s) of your choice.

7. Here is a delightful trio by Jakob Regnart in which parallel thirds and sixths are used continually, and many parallel triads as well, in a popular homophonic style typical of the villanella of the late Sixteenth Century.
Note: The half note remains constant throughout.

Nun Bin Ich Einmal Frei

Jakob Regnart, 16th c.

What is the scale?

This trio will be most effective if both a high choir of two Sopranos and one Alto, and a low choir of two Tenors and a Bass are used, perhaps alternating in A and B, and doubling in C.

Add parts for hand drum and/or triangle or finger cymbals if you wish.

For still more variety of texture, sing the parts an octave lower, with or without recorders doubling the voices.

8. This ancient Easter hymn, **O Filii et Filiae**, in the Aeolian mode, lends itself to a variety of settings using various historical techniques.

8ⓐ Unison

Let us first sing it in unison, doubling in as many octaves as possible.
Note the shifting rhythm of 6 to 3 and back again, as the word accent requires.
Again, playing in octaves.

O Filii et Filiae

17th c. France

8ⓑ Organum

The earliest technique based on the variety of natural ranges in the human voice was Organum, the use of parallel fourths and fifths between the octaves, like this example.
Sing in your comfortable range.
Then try various instrumental combinations.

Continue, being careful to avoid diminished fifths.

8ⓒ Faux Bourdon

The technique of singing in parallel first-inversion chords developed next, like this:

Sometimes a pedal point or drone was added on the tonal center as well, in this case a low **G** on a cello or bass krummhorn or organ.

8ⓓ Heterophony

Melodic ornamentation, as far as we can tell, was Heterophony, the simultaneous decoration of a tune on a high instrument with the playing of the tune in its original simple form, like this:

ⓓ

continue...

8ⓔ Parallel thirds and sixths over a bass line

The tune is also effective in a more conventional setting with parallel thirds and sixths over a simple bass line like this:

Take turns with your partner improvising the second part or improvising a simple bass line for the rest of the song.

8ⓕ Shifting Chords

Another possibility is the use of shifting chords under the tune.

What two chords could you use without requiring any chromatic alterations of the Aeolian mode?

8ⓖ Tonic drone

Another possibility would be to play and sing the verses in octaves - and the choruses in Organum or Faux Bourdon - over a tonic drone.

This would preserve the contrast of solo and tutti typical of this type of early processional carol.

Lesson 9

The Subdominant
Improvisation in Faux Bourdon
Improvising over AX chord patterns
Improvised Dorian dance over I - IV - V

1. Echo what you hear in **B♭** Major on Soprano and Tenor recorder.
   Again, on Alto and Bass.
   Take turns being the leader for four phrases in a row, repeating any phrase that needs it.

2. Play the scale of **B♭** Major in Faux Bourdon (first inversion), with Tenor (or Bass) on low **D**, Alto II on low **F**, and Alto I on **B♭**.
   Again, with Soprano I, Soprano II, and Alto doubling an octave higher.

3. With either or both high and low choirs in Faux Bourdon, follow the leader's hand-sign directing of the <u>upper</u> part.
   Always maintain the same distance between the parts and move in stepwise progressions.
   Repeat tones as needed and change directions at will to make a flowing melody, like this:

4. Again, with chords in Root Position: Bass recorder on **B♭**, Tenor on low **D**, and Alto on low **F**.
   Take turns directing hand signs for the bottom part.

5. Practice the following chord patterns, and name the chords **I**, **IV**, or **V**.

   - What is the common tone between **I** and **IV**? _______
   - Between **I** and **V**? _______
   - Between **IV** and **V**? _______

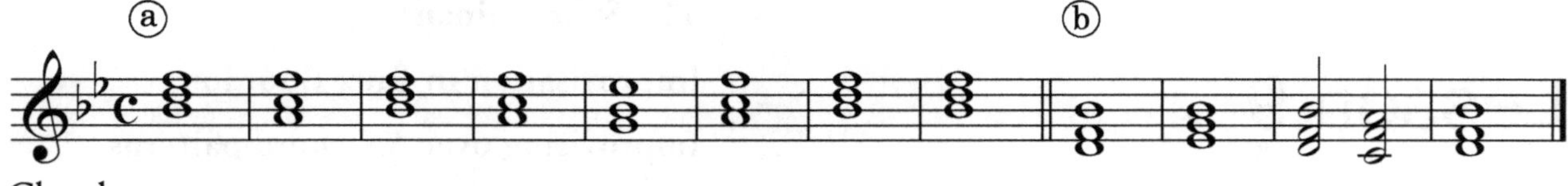

Chords:

6. Take turns improvising a melody over the chord pattern of your choice, beginning with broken-chord tunes and gradually introducing more passing and neighboring tones.
   Note: Since the chords are not rhythmically interesting, try to introduce rhythmic interest into your tunes, no matter how simple, for contrast and continuity.

7. Sing and play the following two-part canon, and learn it by heart.

   Then transpose it to

   - **C** Major
   - **D** Major
   - **F** Major, and
   - **G** Major.

8. Work out a simple bass line for each of the following two tunes, **Old Jubiter** and **A Trumpet Air.** If you have them, use three timpani, tuned to roots of the tonic, subdominant, and dominant chords. Make the bass line rhythmically interesting and fun to play.

Old Jubiter

American Fiddle Tune

A Trumpet Air

Scotland, 18th c.

Form: A A B B

9. With your partner take turns improvising over the following chordal patterns:

10. Work out a simple bass part to conform with the obvious harmonic structure of this little dance.
    Assign parts to the recorders of your choice.
    Add one or two unpitched percussion instruments if you wish.

Dance for Recorders

Isabel Carley

11. With your partner, work out a C section for the **Dance for Recorders** in **D** Dorian, improvising over a **I - IV - V** chordal pattern on AX of your own devising.

Play the entire dance.

Lesson 10

Decoration of the Third

Chaconne

Completing a Rondo for Recorders

1. Another historical improvisatory technique was what Carl Orff called "Umterzen" - playing around with thirds.
Decoration of the third was much used in the later Renaissance period, particularly in music for the lute and for the keyboard.
In its simplest form it is a matter of filling in the thirds in a melody over open fifths, like the examples below. (See Murray, **Orff-Schulwerk Music for Children** Volumes IV and V.)

see Murray, Volume IV, pp 118 ff

see Murray, Volume V, pp 33 ff

2. Improvise similar melodies over the following basses, and write down the best ones here:

3. Probably the most familiar tune in this style of decorated thirds is **Greensleeves**. Here it is in its Dorian version over descending open fifths. (The tune is similar to **Greensleeves and Yellow Lace** in Lesson 6, but the B section melodies vary significantly.)

   Once it is familiar, take turns improvising variations of increasing elaborateness over the same basic accompanying pattern.

Greensleeves

England, 16th c.

4. Here is an authentic example of the decorated-thirds style from Diego Ortiz's famous treatise on ornamentation and other technical problems on the viols, published in Rome in 1545. This is from **Recercada Primera.** (Diego Ortiz, **Tratado de Glosas sobre clausulas y otros generos de Puntos en la Musica de Violones**, Roma, 1553, Bärenreiter Ausgabe 684.)

Recercada Primera (excerpt)

Diego Ortiz, 1545

5. Another example of the same technique occurs in Ortiz's **Chaconne.** (A chaconne is a series of variations over the same harmonic pattern.) These excerpts are taken from **Recercada Quinta.**

   Note: The chord pattern continues throughout excerpts [A] - [E].

Chaconne, Recercada Quinta (excerpts A - E)

Diego Ortiz, 1545

6. Improvise your own Chaconne in the same style.
   - Work out these same chord sequences from the Ortiz excerpt in Step 5, using two or three Orff instruments of your choice.
   - Change the meter as you see fit.
   - Write your theme and two or three variations below.
   - Note: With three or four friends, make an audio recording of the instrumental patterns, for individual practice.
   - Be prepared to play one or two sections in class.
   - Which minor mode will you use? _______
   - Which recorder? _______

Chaconne

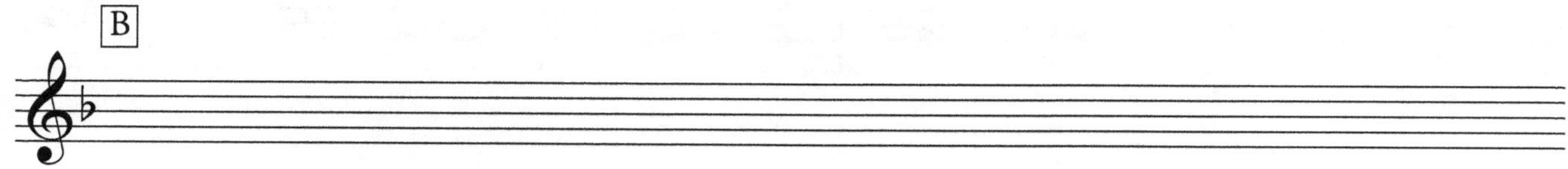

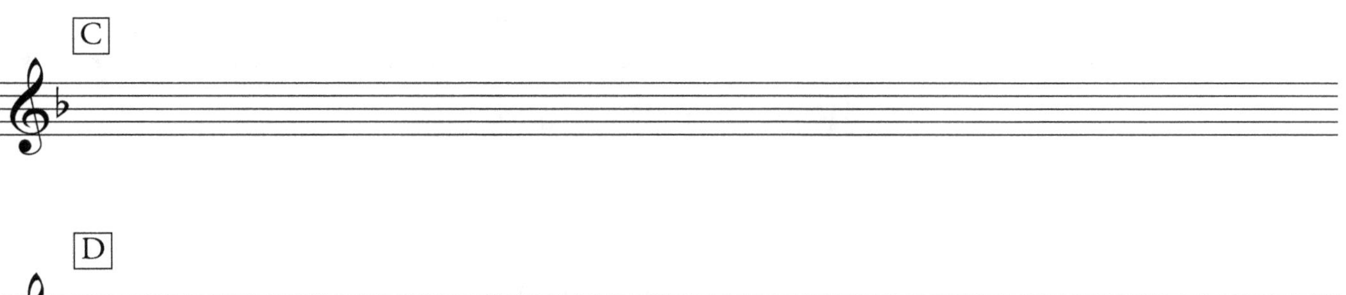

7. Take turns with your partner improvising a new chord pattern on BX.
   - Use three mallets.
   - Improvise a theme and variations over the harmonic pattern.

   Which tonalities best fit the bar instruments?

8. Over the open fifths on Tenor and Bass recorders in the example here, take turns improvising melodies with decorated thirds.

   Write your best one below.

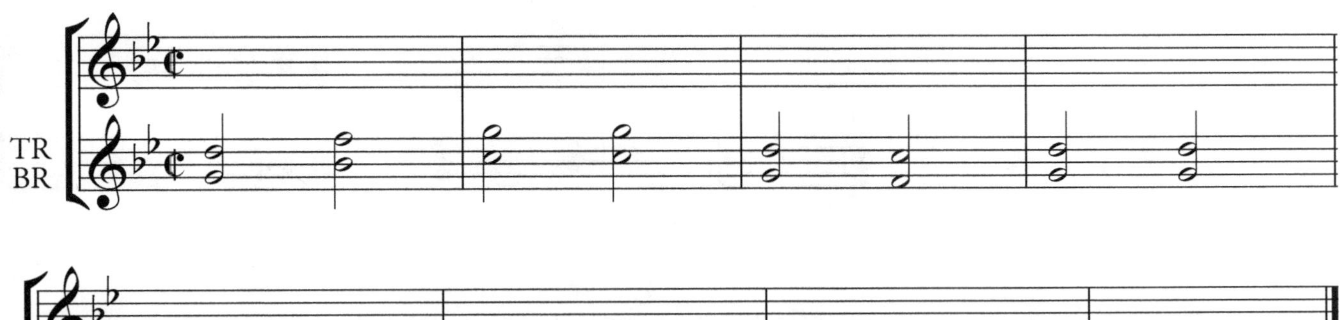

9. Again, using a different scale, and an increasingly complicated melody departing more and more from the simple third patterns and introducing more extended scale and melismatic turns of phrase, like this:

Rondo for Recorders

Isabel Carley and . . . .

Improvise a tune in whichever mode you choose for the B section:

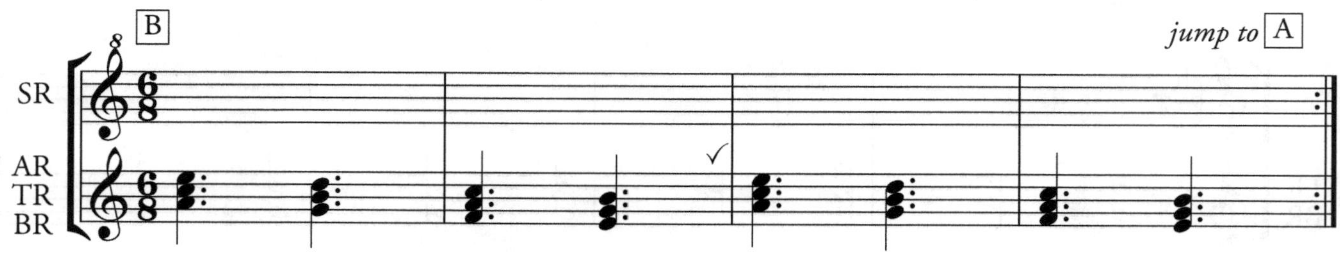

Work out your own C section, over your own bass line, for either recorders or Orff instruments, with a Da Capo to the A section.

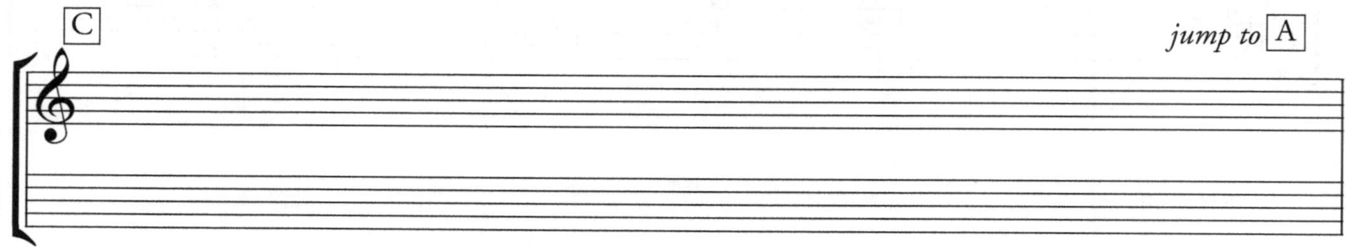

Put our **Rondo for Recorders** together.

Lesson 11

Making Descants
Doubling the descant in thirds or sixths
Using sevenths and ninths

1. Familiar folk tunes may also be decorated with improvised descants. Descants are independent melodies sung or played above the main theme, over its harmonic and rhythmic structure.

We'll start with diatonic scalewise figures in the descant like this:

Au Claire de la Lune

Take turns with your practice partner making up similar stepwise descants for this tune.
Which instruments will play the tune? ________
The descant? ________

2. Work out two descants for this folk song:
   - One with moving stepwise figures, like the descant in Step 1.
   - Another with more rhythmic vitality and punctuation to mark the phrases.
   - Add a bass part for BX or cello.
   - Be prepared to play your work for the class.

The Animal Song

3. This historical descant technique is particularly appropriate in setting early modal tunes like these. Work out decants for each tune, and write them below, indicating the instrumentation and articulation you have in mind.
   Mark the appropriate chords and improvise a bass part for BX, BM, or cello.

Uns Kommt Ein Schiff

German, 13th or 14th c.

Chords:

Marienruf

Augsburg, 1512

4. Occasionally, such a descant may be doubled in thirds or sixths, like this:

Los Cuatro Muleros

Spain

5. Such descants introduce many passing dissonances.
   In some settings, dissonance is deliberately used for expressive effect, often over a pedal point in the bass, like the C Section in this **Time Change Dance Two**.
   Note: Instrumentation and clef change at the B Section.

Time Change Dance Two

Isabel Carley

Form: A B A C A

Lesson 12

Improvisation for Movement
Accompanying movement
Improvisation for dramatic situations
Free solo improvisation over Klang-Ostinato
Unmetered free solo improvisation
Group improvisation

1. The recorder is often used to accompany movement, sometimes following the movement, sometimes leading. Take turns with your partner in improvising in any scale you choose to accompany each other's improvised movement. You might begin with very legato movement in place, such as is used in mirror exercises.

2. Again, using a different scale, make the phrases of unequal lengths.

3. Working with another pair of partners, take turns improvising Q+A phrases in movement and melody simultaneously. Take turns asking and answering the questions in both media.

4. Again, in a different scale:
   Make the answers longer than the questions.
   Then the questions longer than the answers.

5. Improvise answers to the following questions, taking care to match the scale in each case. Choose your favorite, and use it as the A section of an A B A form in which your melody determines the movement in the A sections and your partner's movement determines the melody in the B section.

6. Work out the melody for a simple skipping dance in **A** Dorian, and write it here:

Skipping Dance

7. Work out two or three variations of your skipping dance, with specific movements or movement combinations in mind, such as a slow processional, a waltz, a polka, a time-change dance.
   Change the mode as well, if you wish.
   Try your variations out with your partner, taking turns moving to the melodies without telling each other what you had in mind. Write your favorite below:

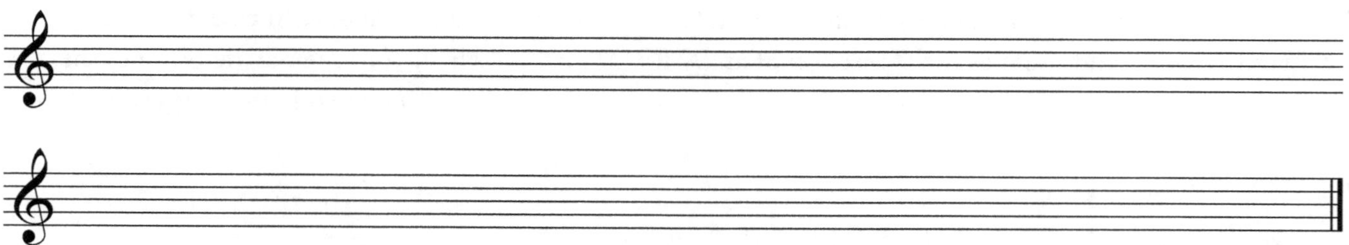

8. In small groups, practice building up bordun and ostinato figures that complement each other, filling in the rhythmic "holes" the other patterns leave. When the patterns are together to your satisfaction, take turns improvising over them on Soprano or Alto recorder, and moving to the music.

9. Set up the bar instruments for **D** Pentatonic. Work out a set of complementary accompanying patterns, as above, using at least three instruments, and take turns improvising on your recorder in your own Q+A phrases.

10. Change the meter and the pentatonic mode, and build the accompanying patterns to match. Then, with three volunteers, play Q+A, Same Q + Different A, over the ensemble. Again, with movement Q+A phrases by three volunteers to match the music. Use at least the *La* and *Re* pentatonic scales. What notes would you use in *La* Pentatonic based on the scale of **D**? _______ In *Re* Pentatonic? _______

11. Practice by yourself improvising in **B♭** Pentatonic. When you find a tune you like, use it as the [A] section for an improvised rondo. Change the pentatonic mode in each of the episodes between repetitions of [A] if you can.

12. Build an accompaniment with at least three bar instruments with **D** as the tonal center, keeping them simple and unspecific as to scale, at least in the two lower parts. Take turns improvising, over the same accompaniment, in
    - Partial Pentatonic
    - Full Pentatonic
    - *La, Re,* and *So* Pentatonic
    - Dorian
    - Aeolian
    - Mixolydian
    - Major
    - Minor (with raised seventh).

13. Improvisation over rhythmic ostinati is also very effective for accompanying movement, or simply by itself. Take turns with your partner doing the following body percussion or drum patterns and improvising over them on Soprano, Alto, Tenor, or Sopranino, in a variety of modes and major scales.

BODY PERCUSSION:

14. Improvise in the appropriate mode or key over the following patterns:

15. Recorder improvisation is often used to accompany movement in a dramatic setting. Imagine, for instance, the scene in which Goldilocks goes skipping gaily off into the forest, stopping now and then to pick flowers or blackberries as she goes deeper and deeper into the forest, and make up an extended melody to accompany her movement. What meter and key will you choose?

16. Choose your own dramatic interlude from a fairy or folk tale, and write your tune below. Add unpitched percussion if you need it to help establish the mood, and indicate the tempo and dynamics you desire.

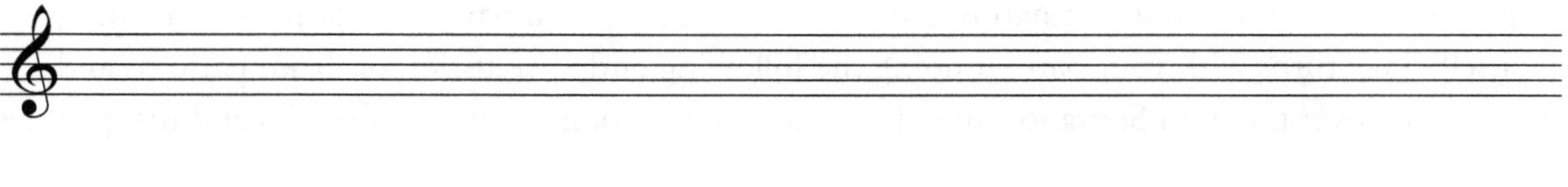

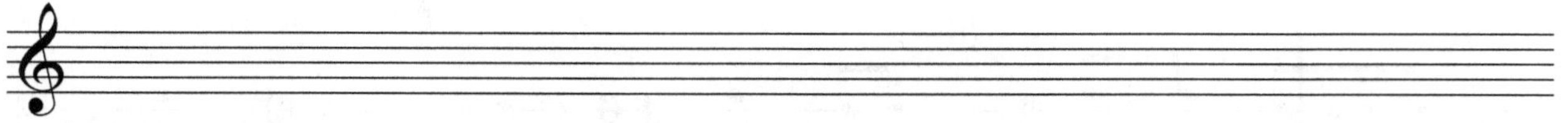

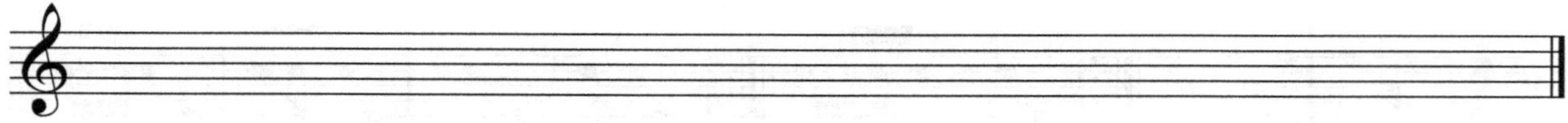

17. Another type of improvisation resembles vocal recitative, and may be combined with it in story-telling, particularly in interludes between scenes. It may also be purely instrumental, over a carpet of sound. With this kind of accompaniment, there is a regular pulse over which the melody moves freely in irregular figures and phrases. Sometimes such an accompaniment is divided between different instruments in a Klang-Ostinato or sound pattern like this:

Isabel Carley

AR
SG
AX
AM
FC
Vc

Try inventing your own Klang-Ostinati with a group of five or six, and take turns improvising over the accompaniment on your Alto recorder. Practice with your partner too, using the Alto Metallophone to provide the pulse, and taking turns at both assignments. Keep changing the mode or key.

18. Another type of solo improvisation is extremely free formally, sometimes unmetered, with irregular note values and frequent ornaments, such as you might invent as an introduction to a Christmas cantata, particularly of the shepherds on the hillside, or as a prelude to an improvised setting of the Twenty-third Psalm, such as this:

Continue, or make up your own.

19. Group Improvisation may also be explored, using any of the separate techniques we have considered, or combining them. For example:

- In the *La* Pentatonic scale of **B♭**, build accompanying patterns with at least three bar instruments, and improvise as a group on your recorders, subsiding into low-range ostinati or dropping out entirely when your inspiration runs out, picking up other people's ideas, or developing your own, as the texture demands, within the set scale. (**G B♭ C D F**)
- Let a volunteer work out a shifting-chord pattern on BX or AX; Bass, Tenor, and Alto II double or adapt the chord pattern; and a group of volunteers improvise on Soprano and Alto. Choose a major scale first, and use patterns with shifts from **I - II** or from **I - VI**. Try modes and minors later, shifting from **I - VII** or from **I - III**.
- Choose a simple harmonic pattern, such as [**I - I - V - V** | **I - I - V - I**] or [**I - I - IV - IV** | **I - I - V - I**], and build it up in the ensemble. Let volunteers improvise on recorders (and/or with voices), joining in when they're ready, until everyone's participating.
- Work out a Chaconne figure with the instruments, and let a volunteer improvise a four-phrase melody, to be joined by more volunteers in each new four-phrase unit until the whole group is playing.

20. Experiment with new combinations of group and solo improvisation, with definite assignments of scale and form, whenever you can. Or, on a large project, give group assignments for different sections, to be worked out and brought back to class for a combined performance. This division of assignments is particularly good in dramatic projects, particularly when time is limited. Choose a fairy tale, divide it into scenes, one for each group, and let the group members themselves volunteer for the various roles and assignments.

Fingerings for Recorders in F *and* C

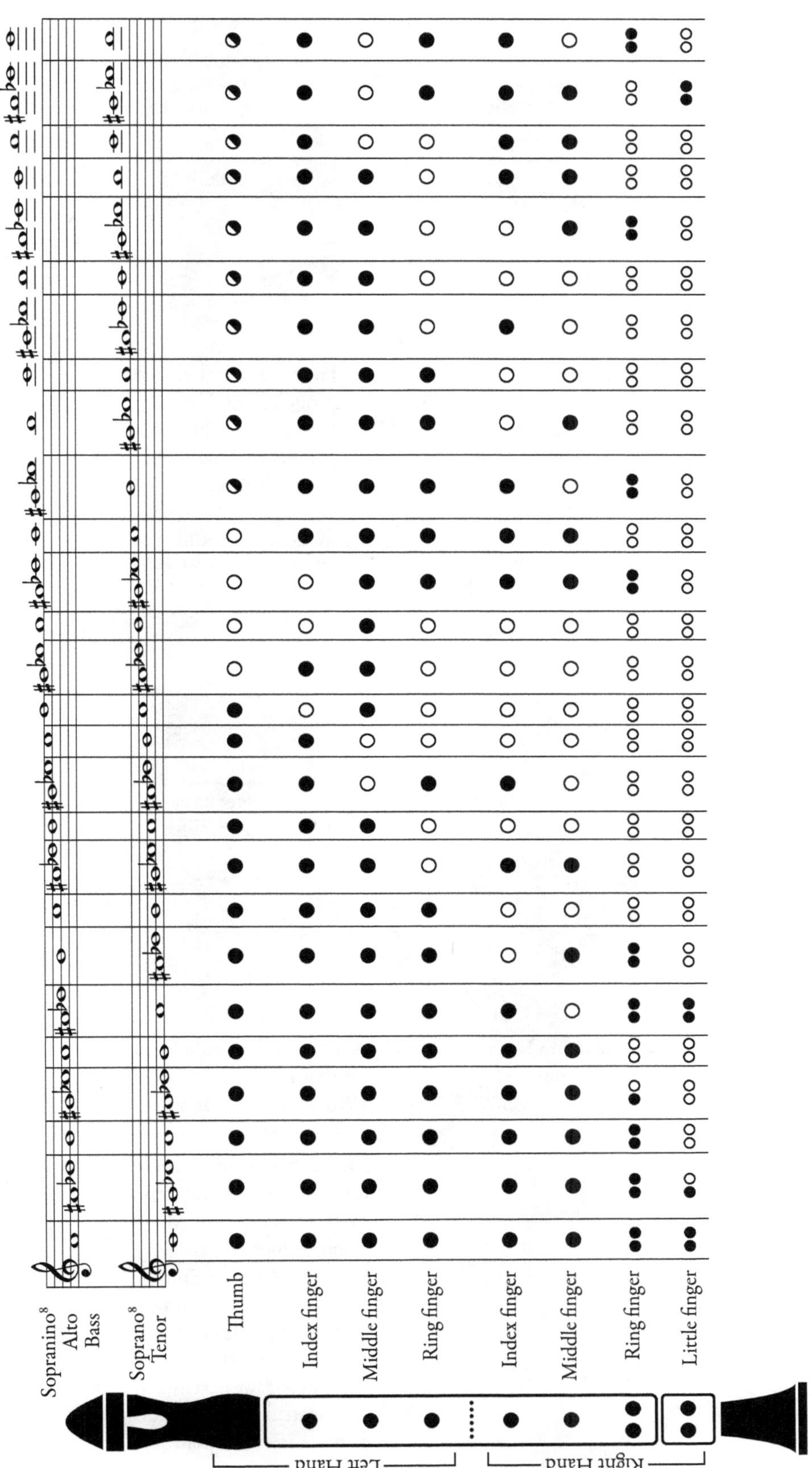

Brasstown Press Editions

Isabel McNeill Carley Orff Essentials Collection

Eleven lessons for beginners and their teachers that explore C, G, and F Pentatonic and related modes on the soprano recorder. 46 songs and introductory exercises.
wire-o ISBN 978-1-931922-46-3
paperback ISBN 978-0-9836545-0-6

Building on RIT One, RIT Two transfers soprano fingering patterns to the alto recorder and introduces hexatonic and diatonic major and minor modes. 52 songs and intermediate exercises.
wire-o ISBN 978-1-931922-07-4
paperback ISBN 978-0-9836545-1-3

For the student already proficient on both C and F recorders. These lessons parallel the material in the Orff Schulwerk (volumes III and V). 46 challenging songs for advanced students.
wire-o ISBN 978-1-93192208-1
paperback ISBN 978-0-9836545-2-0

IM Carley's written work from over thirty years. The essays are grouped in three sections: Origins, Practicum, and Exhortations. Includes biographical sketch and list of IMC's publications.
ISBN 978-0-9836545-3-7

IMC's Five Little Books

41 Songs in G Pentatonic Scale and Modes.
ISBN 978-0-9836545-6-8

47 Songs in C Pentatonic and F Pentatonic.
ISBN 978-0-9836545-7-5

44 Songs. Expanded ranges, Pentatonic to Diatonic.
ISBN 978-0-9836545-8-2

The three My Recorder Reader books are a coordinated series of songs to bring a student from elementary playing to a more experienced level. Notes are added one by one to extend the student's range, with minimal instructional comments. The carefully graduated sequence of the pieces facilitates individual mastery and skill development.

My Song Primer — Isabel McNeill Carley — 13 Songs & Lessons

13 Songs, one per lesson, from So-Mi to Pentatonic.
ISBN 978-0-9836545-4-4

35 Songs in 6 Lessons, D-E-G-A range.
ISBN 978-0-9836545-5-1

Establish a secure musical foundation with the step-by-step lessons offered in My Song Primer (for singing) and My Recorder Primer (for soprano recorder). Songs are interwoven in lessons with speech and rhythm exercises, suggestions for percussion and Orff instruments, and ideas for games and movement.

EBOOK!

All new essays and articles plus a read-aloud story.
ISBN 978-0-9836545-9-9

Brasstown Press ⊘ brasstownpress@gmail.com ⊘ brasstownpress.com

www.ingramcontent.com/pod-product-compliance
Lightning Source LLC
Chambersburg PA
CBHW050503110426
42742CB00018B/3360

* 9 7 8 0 9 8 3 6 5 4 5 2 0 *